SANTA
TARANTULA

THE ANDRÉS MONTOYA POETRY PRIZE

2004, *Pity the Drowned Horses*, Sheryl Luna
Final Judge: Robert Vasquez

2006, *The Outer Bands*, Gabriel Gomez
Final Judge: Valerie Martínez

2008, *My Kill Adore Him*, Paul Martínez Pompa
Final Judge: Martín Espada

2010, *Tropicalia*, Emma Trelles
Final Judge: Silvia Curbelo

2012, *A Tongue in the Mouth of the Dying*, Laurie Ann Guerrero
Final Judge: Francisco X. Alarcón

2014, *Furious Dusk*, David Campos
Final Judge: Rhina P. Espaillat

2016, *Of Form & Gather*, Felicia Zamora
Final Judge: Edwin Torres

2018, *The Inheritance of Haunting*, Heidi Andrea Restrepo Rhodes
Final Judge: Ada Limón

2022, *Stepmotherland*, Darrel Alejandro Holnes
Final Judge: John Murillo

2024, *Santa Tarantula*, Jordan Pérez
Final Judges: Alexandra Lytton Regalado and Sheila Maldonado

The Andrés Montoya Poetry Prize, named after the late California native and author of the award-winning book, *The Iceworker Sings*, supports the publication of a first book by a Latino or Latina poet. Awarded every other year, the prize is administered by Letras Latinas—the literary program of the Institute for Latino Studies at the University of Notre Dame.

SANTA
TARANTULA

Jordan Pérez

University of Notre Dame Press
Notre Dame, Indiana

Published by the University of Notre Dame Press
Notre Dame, Indiana 46556
undpress.nd.edu

Library of Congress Control Number: 2023946670

ISBN: 978-0-268-20751-9 (Hardback)
ISBN: 978-0-268-20752-6 (Paperback)
ISBN: 978-0-268-20753-3 (WebPDF)
ISBN: 978-0-268-20750-2 (Epub3)

For all who cling to the light

CONTENTS

II. DISSENT

III. GOSPEL

ACKNOWLEDGMENTS

An abundance of gratitude to all who came before, to those making my life rich now, to my teachers and collaborators, to Eden, to Bailey, to the University of Notre Dame Press team, to Alexandra Lytton Regalado and Sheila Maldonado—who chose this book for the Andrés Montoya Prize—to Francisco Aragon, to my SOSA team, and to all who look for the light . . . even in the darkest places.

A handful of these poems have appeared previously:

"Santa Tarantula"—Winner, 2019 Cosmonauts Avenue Poetry Prize; *Poetry*

"Deadgirl"—Finalist, 2021 Joy Harjo Poetry Prize

"Body"—*Mississippi Review*

"Smallmouth" and "Shell"—Finalist, 2022 Poetry International Prize

"O God of Cuba" and "Mixed-Up Sestina"—*Poetry*

INTRODUCTION TO THE POEMS

Jordan Pérez's *Santa Tarantula* is no coy and demure debut. It comes to us urgent and dauntless. "It demands to be / known," says Pérez in the first poem, "Smallmouth," how "[t]he dance / or the fight," of the smallmouth bass pulled onto the dock serves as the opening image of her collection and embodies the survival of all that is feminine. With poems about desire and devouring, hunger and satisfaction, violence and resistance, Pérez dedicates this book "for all who cling to the light" and so invites us into that light as witnesses of women's pain, persistence, and resilience.

Divided into three sections, the lyrical poems of *Santa Tarantula* follow a dreamlogic embedded with rich details and are guided by revelatory proclamations of atonement and reckoning. Set in the low-country South of loam and terroir cut with palmetto and cicadas, Pérez's poems also return to the forced labor camps and sugarcane fields of 1960s Cuba. Pérez recognizes wounds old and new, discovering along the way sliver scars and shards as she braids her experiences with those of her ancestors, including her grandfather who lived through the hunger and torture of the masculinity camps, and reveals "two generations / of quiet // sucking each other's pain / as you might a snakebite."

Pérez assembles her poems as shadowboxes, curious collections of the natural world threaded with biblical tales and family memories. The stories of Lot and his daughter, Samson and Delilah, and other stories less commonly written about, including those of Hosea, Gomer, and Ruhamah, and Jael and Heber, are presented as persona poems and sometimes with variations, posing alternative endings that consider how they could've played out differently. *Santa Tarantula* speaks of women's roles and the perceived idea of "ladyness" and how a woman is expected to conduct herself. Pérez's poems are a poised and alert call to give attention to the violence against women; in "Deadgirl" she invokes the image of a soft mushroom pushing through leaves and says: "I believed it was the knee of a dead girl, / [and] was furious with her for being so vulnerable." The speaker also presents examples of confident women, her mother who fights her sisters to eat the chicken-heart, who "takes / communion with her eyes open," and who teaches her daughter how to float.

At times Pérez's quiet observation reminds us of Ada Limón, with the compactness of Louise Glück, but Pérez stands out, a remarkable and confident voice that understands survival is in the telling:

> ... I refuse
> to die ...
> ... having not come into the fullness of myself,
> having not said this is my blood. This, my body. Saying no
> or yes, and liking it.

Paralleled with a nature redolent with larkspurs, wet oaks, and oleander, the speaker explores her body and sexuality. Embedded throughout the poems are Pérez's unique yoking of words—"bruisebelt," "saltneck," "breaththiefs," "rhinoskinned," "moonsoft"—creating painterly images in surreal landscapes. The poems convey want and hunger and are fragrant with the smell of trampled grapes, rose syrup, and tobacco, of wrists dotted with orchid sap, of the "guayaba's split red belly." The speaker considers the presence of her body in the world; in "Misplaced" she searches and finds:

> ... My clavicle
> is buried under the wilting
> lilies by the sink. My hip bone gleams
> under a stranger's coffee cup.

And in the poem "Bathymetry" she leaps from the desire of "mermaids roiling / under the water" to an image that is so plainly grounded, "I sometimes leave the potatoes / unwashed or the corn still streaked with hair —/ wanting the wildness inside me, too." In a voice as haunting as the furred backs of tarantulas, Pérez reclaims her wildness.

As co-juror, Sheila Maldonado concluded of Pérez's work, "She approaches all possible sites of destruction for the feminine with particular, devastating clarity; her poems like small resurrections." I will also continue to be visited upon by Pérez's poems. She gives praise to the sensorial world, looks deep, and asks to be seen. In the poem "Dissent" she is "fists raised   legs planted   young teeth / cursing." In "This Is What the Girl Really Wants," she says: "I offer myself the washed fruit, / and accept it from myself." Pérez sings "the alto parts," letting go of shame and "curtseying only to herself." Visceral and glistening, Pérez's *Santa Tarantula* is a brave and searing debut.

— ALEXANDRA REGALADO LYTTON
March 1, 2023
San Salvador, El Salvador

I

SMALLMOUTH

Smallmouth

It demands to be
known. The gnats
in their conductor's
dance. The extra leaves
in the table. The mole
belly-up in the pool.
The unchoked sob.
The white pants hidden
beneath the bed. The daffodil's
hand from the dead.
The one occupied room.
The frog in the middle
of the kitchen. The strange face
in the mirror. The whiskey
in the underwear drawer.
The gasp in the sink drain.
The girl's shirt
behind the shed. The trampled
lemon balm. The dance
or the fight. The bitter walnut
in the stomach. The smallmouth
bass on the dock. You are more
wife than my wife
says your father.

Twelve

First, the stomach, like a balloon.
You take your bike to see the doctor,
who presses her hands to her mouth.

She looks like your mother,
as all women look like your mother
when they cry.

Then, the baby, as unrecognizable
as the squirm on the wand.
Then, the baby.

On the bus, you sit in the front.
You nod solemnly to the women
who have paused their gossiping.

You are not lost, just visiting.
You cross your legs like a lady.
You press your mouth like a lady.

Your Father Knew Many Women

And they flourished,
his apricot grove.
Glowing after dark, they webbed
together in soft gossips.
They were themselves
hungry. You'll call them lonely, or sad,
but you can't say which you hoped to be
true. The summer you turned twelve,
you thought of little else but how he was
an excellent farmer. Apricots will take
whatever they can get if they are truly
hungry enough.
You said you understood the situation.
There is nothing like a man
with slender hands.
You visited them to ask
what he was like, to check
them for scrapes from the large borer
bug. You carried a salve at all times.

On the bus, an old woman cradles
something in a brown paper bag.
You wait for the briny scream of fish
or the glow of an egg tart,
but all she is holding is her own hand.

The Masculinity Camps

Gay men and maybe-gay men and dissidents
were sent. The national ballet lost ten, many priests
were rounded up, writers. My grandfather, yes.
As the buses left, women threw themselves to hang
onto the sides, overlapping like palm fronds.
The men were taught to shoot into the trees (like men),
the dirt (like men), a sleeping man (an unavoidable
accident). Some were shocked and killed themselves.
My grandfather's camp was never given a name.
The sign at the front only said, "work will make you men."
It was repeated daily, like a catechism. One boy,
not even grown, refused to work the fields.
With a bayonet, a soldier cut a red sash into his body.

Deadgirl

There was the time a soft mushroom broke
through the thick of the leaves on the lawn
and I believed it was the knee of a dead girl,
was furious with her for being so vulnerable.

The next morning, after the rain, deadgirl knees
were everywhere. Who was there to tell?
I watched these girls become part of the earth.
A woman is known by the silence she keeps.

I could not stop thinking of my own ladyness,
could never remember if that meant to be easy
or always out of grasp, the way I couldn't be sure
which house in the neighborhood held the man

who touched little girls, and so in every house
is the man who touches little girls.

Knockout Rose

There is nothing but this
moment of purple October
with its fertile dusks.

The thrips have paused
to watch the oaks wetten.
The larkspurs have come

into their roundness. Can you
feel the pines flirt with the light?
Would you brush a little onto my face?

I arch against your palm
until you cannot look away.
Somehow, this has become

our normal. A young girl
might do anything
for a hint of light on her face.

In This Story

Maybe in this story, the girl hears the crow.

Maybe she hears the crow and looks around.

Maybe she hears the crow and looks around and takes the safe way home.

Maybe she hears the crow and looks around and takes the safe way home and doesn't smile at the man in the blue hat.

Maybe she hears the crow and looks around and takes the safe way home and doesn't smile at the man in the blue hat or does smile at the man in the blue hat if that's safer.

Maybe she hears the crow and looks around and takes the safe way home and doesn't smile at the man in the blue hat or does smile at the man in the blue hat if that's safer and walks with purpose (the purpose being not getting killed).

Maybe she hears the crow and looks around and takes the safe way home and doesn't smile at the man in the blue hat or does smile at the man in the blue hat if that's safer and walks with purpose (the purpose being not getting killed) and pretends to get a call from her boyfriend.

Maybe she hears the crow and looks around and takes the safe way home and doesn't smile at the man in the blue hat or does smile at the man in the blue hat if that's safer and walks with purpose (the purpose being not getting killed) and pretends to get a call from her boyfri

Body

sorry to say it   I almost forgot to keep on living
one winter so thin   it grabbed its own shoulder blades

I kept having to stretch up   pull myself from oak trees
thick with birds   where I waved like an inflatable dancer

eventually I came to know   the most likely storm drains
the quietest alleyways   to hide my own body

shallots wilted on their stems   unpicked
I stopped planning for summer   gave away my clothes

they gave my mother her thyroid   in a plastic jar
floating like a fat date   she forgot to bring the rest of herself

she shaved off her hair   thick in the drain she burrowed
in her closet   like a crushed winter coat   she and I

we sing the alto parts   nice girls don't ask for solos
fill our pockets with hydrangeas   tell a man to touch us

there are so many expendable parts   viscid eggs
silkworm appendix   fisted spleen

in a park   to my neck in sandbox   I thought how easy
to duck a little deeper   no body left to lose

The Men

The one who force-feeds women
other women, the one who makes
butter for breakfast in a mason jar,
The one who amputates women's
legs and sews them onto other
victims, the one who threads neat patches
into the toes of your socks, the one
who cuts his own name into women's
faces, the one who carves a vegetable garden
into the backyard, the one who surgically removes
lips and keeps them floating in jars, the one
who steeps calendula blossoms in oil for winter,
the one who says *I am not the other men,*
the one who is not the others.

Mixed-Up Sestina

For José

We have been shitting and pissing in the sealed buses through the night,
then out, and stadium lights click on. Rows of stands standing empty.
I think of the stories of ancient Rome: lions or dogs tearing apart
the faithful in arenas like these. Then here, my own shaking hands.
Some say we will be shot at midfield, but no one is sure.
One dancer can't forget his training. Still in first position, this man.

Electric barbed wire makes a soft click sound through the night.
Some say it is turned off during the day, but no one is sure.
We are here to learn to be men, so we rip out the grass with our hands.
The man beside me, whose shoe is untied, cries to himself "Apart
from God, nothing" again and again. I suddenly feel like a man
who has returned from a trip to find his entire town empty.

We are even given a new alphabet. M for Marxism. R for Raúl. Apart
from this, a test: Walk until the soldier believes you are not a gay man.
There is no rice. The boat has not come from China. The empty
dishes could be my own wife's dishes, so delicate in my hands.
Some say the ungrateful are stabbed with their own forks, but no one is sure.
Beside me, a painter with blistering palms who once did fine work.

They cut the stubborn ones with bayonets. We continue killing the grass, man
after man kneeling. The victory still marked on the scoreboard sits empty.
Someone says the umpires were very unfair that day, but no one is sure.
Many have lost their shoes, and so steal others until no one can tell his apart
from anyone else's. A lawyer tries to make a point by sitting on his hands.
After we hear him die I can no longer sleep through the night.

We are brought to uproot fields thick with marabú until our hands
are covered in blood and thorns. I wonder if the Jehovah's Witness thinks man
should be grateful to suffer as Jesus did. Carnations sprout in an empty
patch, but nobody seems to notice. Even together we are apart.
Castro inspects our work. The chicken he brought for his supper squawks until
    night.
Someone says he will soon move to reduce numbers, but no one is sure.

We stop caring and sleep on the dormitory ground, curled man to man.
The limestone soil is empty. The cottontail's eyes are empty.
I cannot stop shaking as I pull the root and its own earth apart.
I remember the time my father and I sang by the sea long into the night.
I remember the morning when a frog sunbathed in my cupped hands.
I think my daughters would still know me now, but I cannot be sure.

When Judah saw her, he thought she was a prostitute,
for she had covered her face. Not realizing that she was his
daughter-in-law, he went over to her by the roadside
and said, "Come now, let me sleep with you."

—Genesis 38:15–16

Tamar

I never knew that a veil could envelop a man.
My facelessness is dazzling, my wrists
dark aperitifs. He stumbles in the dirt

like a child, this father. The city gate is teeming
with other women's fathers who do not nose
at their wrists as mine does. He tugs my sleeve

like a child. This father offers one young goat
to have his fill. His hands flutter with yearning.
It is known that prostitutes do not cry before men.

Like a child, this frecklenosed father weeps in my arms.
When our son is born his wrist blooms first, and
like his father, this child pulls himself back into me.

Her brother Absalom said to her, "Has that Amnon, your brother,
been with you? Be quiet for now, my sister; he is your brother.
Don't take this thing to heart." And Tamar lived in her brother
Absalom's house, a desolate woman.

—2 Samuel 13:20

A Desolate Woman

In the palace, incense gleams rich
from shallow dishes. In a bedroom,
soft elbowed women tremble
around my brother. He calls for bread
and they flutter, careening through the hall
like great salmon.

But I am told to carry it, as he would like to watch.
And here is the dark childface that once
flung me, frozen with laughter, above his head.
He is slippery now against my hip.
He rakes away the flour on my arm.
Through this gourdbright breaking,
there is my own hand, steady against a table.

It is perfect, as if waiting to be painted.

Men Everywhere Are Setting Traps

The sea is an incarnation of God.
God is quiet. By the lowcountry moan of the docks,
the crabs run through the underwater grasses.
In the reflected world, the men approach

with the wire traps swaying before them.
The lures, chicken necks choked with string.
The terroir, peeling palmettos and the shoreline,
as abrupt as the silence after a scream.

The men's amusing experiment: to see if the right-
hand claw, removed, might grow back. Their trick:
to hold the legs and stroke the head—putting
the flailing crab to sleep makes things simpler.

(Some of the crab women, heavy with egg sponge,
will be tossed until they're desirable again.)
What a creature, who can be fully sucked away and still
leave behind her little life-
like shell.

The Glory Has Departed

My mother sucks sardines from the tin, absorbs
them into her own soft body. You can almost
disappear sideways, she says, standing before
the hotel mirror in knee socks, broaches clinging
to her slip like cicadas. We take a train to Cinque Terre,
scatter fists of loam from the windows, insist
that the earth absolve our skin. My mother rubs
flaxseed oil into my palms: this oil of purity
she prays will cleanse me in the Italian sun.
But the glory has departed from my body
and cannot be gathered back.
We buy fists of grapes at an open
air market, partake of the blood.
I watch her after through the shower glass,
smell the thick oleanders wilt,
sense her wild mourning, see
that she has shaved off all her hair.

That night they got their father to drink wine, and the older

daughter went in and slept with him. He was not aware

of it when she lay down or when she got up.

—Genesis 19:33

Lot's Daughter

I never knew I could touch evil,
play with its edges like some wild thing.
I trampled the grapes, pressed the juice
through the hem of my skirt. In the evening,
my father crawls through the cave door,
snuffling like a wild boar. His neckskin is loose,
as if his saltwife sucked away the water
as she died. I feel my uterus begin to crinkle
like his chiffon saltneck. The wine dribbles
through his neck and through my fingers
and he smiles up at me: this disgusting beautiful
fatherface. His mouth is the color of rose syrup.
I hold his body like the son I must have. *Take
my virgin daughter's body*, he had told the wild
village. He does not know me now
through his foam eyes, thrusts upward.
I float to a stalactite, cling there like a sail.
I look down on my body and his body, see
that he clings around my neck.

Letter to My Grandfather in April

I have you to thank
for these inheritances:

a chopped plum
still bleeding;

dark pipe tobacco
leaking from its box,

strung cowrie shells
glistening like virgins.

Papa, your hands are now
my father's hands,

your bruisebelt is his own.
We are running through the wheat

off 78, two generations
of quiet

sucking each other's pain
as you might a snakebite.

My father has thrown his funeral
jacket over the car antenna

and it waits there like an accident.
We pretend to miss its darkness.

We tear apart the wheat,
cry like new mothers.

II

DISSENT

O God of Cuba

O god of tarantulas hissing from the trees
O god of cassava cut to the quick
O god of the chicken's dragging, broken neck
O god of burying your money
O god of guayaba's split red belly
O god of the soldier taking your wedding ring
O god of young cursing teeth
O god of the baseball stadium where,
in 1966, a soldier stood on third base
and sent hundreds of men to work
the sugarcane fields.

O god of barbed wire fences
O god of losing your name
O god of eating stray cats
O god of fake executions
O god of real executions
O god of being hung by your hands
O god of paper flowers in your bunk

Dissent

We sisters knew that the tarantulas in the trees
were sweet and we stroked their fur backs, round abdomens
thrumming against our palms. We knew to pluck
the cassava leaves close to the quick, to soak
the roots in water to kill the toxicity; We knew
that prayers would not return our mother's wedding ring
or our father from a work camp in the mountains.
We knew how to swing our last chicken around our heads
until its neck broke and it ran, head dragging the soil
until we chopped it off. We knew to cry dissent in our bedroom
in whispers, in the manner of our parents, in the stance
of warriors — fists raised   legs planted   young teeth
cursing. We knew, with feet sinking deep into red
limestone soil that we were going to flee Cuba while still
clinging to the trees.

Santa Tarantula

Now we praise her, her soft scopulae
for scaling glass, her silk spinnerets, always
reaching. There is shifting the egg sac often,
which a male arachnologist named brooding.
There is losing babies and calling this
our lives. There is singingsingingsinging, staring
into another mother's face and saying it is still
the sun. Also, bittersweet sea smoke. Also,
burnt sugar hissing on the stove. There is scaphism:
death by milk and honey in a shallow dish.
There is shame surfacing like foam.
There is the most powerful species named *johnnycashi,*
and his hooks there to restrain our fangs during sex.
"If one crawls into my bed and I name it, will it be
nicer to me?" asks one man, as some of us cling
to trees, some to the soil sacristy. Praise
the tarantula woman still alive at forty. Praise her shifting
smalt of sky, her quiet stare, her morning face shriving
the sheets. This is how you kill a tarantula.
Cover her, and hope to God she suffocates.

After putting him to sleep on her lap, she called for someone to shave off the seven braids of his hair, and so began to subdue him. And his strength left him. Then she called,
"Samson, the Philistines are upon you!"

—Judges 16:19–20

Delilah

God forgot to give me sleep.
This puff adder is rhinoskinned
and gentle. He lies glassy
on the loom.
My beloved pulls his hair
across my shoulder
as he sleeps, the thickness
everdark between us.
It nests into my heartbeat.
I cannot help but suck
it into my mouth,
the fir-oiled tail in my teeth.
I cannot help but spread it:
kohled braid across my belly.
I keep waking in the seams
of the town,
coiled around an adder
and her moonsoft eggs.
Each time I return to Samson,
his rhinoskinned back
gleams above the blankets.
I could not live anymore
through adder egg nights
and so this cut away adderhead
rolls from my fingers.
But love, this new sleep
is not worth the killing.

Becoming Wild

My x-rayed tibia arches across its axis in a milk rib curve. There are many sterile curves here: discarded stethoscope, uncoiled bandage, concerned smile of the doctor above my swollen ankle. *I hope the guy looks worse*, she says. I dot my wrists with orchid sap to erase any lingering humanness. The tarantula's heart pumps its colorless blood, having chosen her eggs to be daughters. She knows resilience in the marrow. There is no one to tell about these lilting bones. We are too busy practicing survival.

The Dream

The boys I have loved are gathered and we are having a dinner party. Solomon carves the meat in his dress blues. Ezekiel offers to do the trick with the tablecloth. Gideon pours the bourbon, eyes closed. They eat and eat and each time I bring out a new dish it is devoured before I can sit with them. The boys argue about how long until your body isn't yours anymore. Every four weeks, they say, you have entirely new skin. Every seven years, nearly everything has been turned over. I am pregnant and overjoyed but I keep misplacing my belly.

Gomer conceived again and gave birth to a daughter.
Then the Lord said to Hosea, "Call her Lo-Ruhamah
(which means 'not loved'), for I will no longer show love to Israel,
that I should at all forgive them."

—Hosea 1:6

Gomer

And though I don't mention it
to the others very often,
my luteface shakes to be touched.
The moon has paused, nosy
against the dark. The katydids stare.
My daughter has been given
the name, *Unloved*, and I have
no mouth to choose another.
As I was pulled from Egypt, so
Hosea plants me for himself;
my limbs thick with timid figs.
They cling like folded bats.
I urge them to swell with sugar,
to rest heavy in unloved palms.

———————

"Stand in the doorway of the tent," he told her. "If someone comes
by and asks you, 'Is anyone in there?' say "No." But Jael,
Heber's wife, picked up a tent peg and a hammer and went
quietly to him while he lay fast asleep, exhausted.
She drove the peg through his temple into the ground,
and he died.

—Judges 4:20–21

Jael

I entered this world
without hands
with heavy sleeves
covering nothing.
I watered the stumps
soaked them in the Jordan
in the brack faithfully
and lo
and behold!
flesh filled like a sponge
and nails like new shells
which could hold this skein
of goat's milk, still warm.
Basking in this newness
I stroked the town
left stripes in the dust
left fingerskin
beckoned for Sisera
with the longest finger
he moved to sleep
but these new fingers
were eager for their living
took up the stake
with their own newblood.
I cooed them on
these mewling serpents.
As it was time for supper
they dove for the brainmeat
and were satisfied.

I Consider Violence

When the starvation-hair appears
all over my body, you call it fascinating,
which is not the same as beautiful.
I never decide what to wish for first,
food or you. Or rather, eating food again
or never again eating you. Your favorite part
of me, my cupped hipbone, empty
as a half mango scooped clean of its flesh.
Your least favorite part, my hunger.

I learn to fill myself with other things:
the julienned light in the bedroom, mouthfuls
of Debussy from the old piano, the endless suck
of the toilet, which, bravely, never stops running.
Even vowels become impossible luxuries,
so round they seem indulgent against my tongue.

I consider violence after hearing that on death row
you get one last perfect meal. I imagine the photo
in the newspaper story, where I look so
beautiful.

I think of the woman in the Bible
who asks for John's head on a platter.
Maybe she was only hungry.
Maybe she wanted to be satisfied.

Wanting

In morning I bring Gideon a ginger knot   knobbed with green
but he tosses it   swollen against the carrot shavings   to compost

he waves away the cats   thick on the swept porch
hunched into themselves   he says they are dirty creatures

as am I   and the two become one mind   who has no time for wonder
who does not   languish against the softturned dirt

or fist the cobwebs   lick torn envelope tongues   suck olive pits
we are up to our elbows in soap each day   up to our elbows in alone

I grow suspicious of wanting   turn everything to right angles
sponge mold from the shower grout   claim goodness

then, see it with me   dusk approaching like   trunk fading to branch
limbs dark and veeing   like shouting or diminuendo

wonder at the shadow of a heart's sac   offal for our supper
it curls like a frown   spoked aorta leaking

I ask him to pray to me   in my sleep when I cannot be modest
shrug off my own selfness   and finally the wonderful dark

heavy and smiling   above him I untie my hair   halo
"and the two become one flesh"   wonderful and dirty

I find my own wanting   moondusted with waiting   still bright
in the dark   and the devouring   it is good

New Study Says Men Who Do Dishes Are Less Likely to Kill You

And it is always
the careful man,
his hands brushing
the curved basin
of the sink.
The birds outside,
still and watching.
His rag, a shirt
that was once
torn open. He traces
the syrup thalweg,
the slick
salmon skin,
the strawberry tops
caught in their blush.
He adores each dish
in the light,
as is customary
of good men.
An apricot bobs
to the surface,
asking to be eaten.
He cups it in his hand.
Now, the mug
he accidently bit
in his excitement.
Here, the pan
striped over the years,
which he calls
perfect. This is

undoubtedly a wet business,
but he has eaten
and eaten, so it is right.
Even the sun is here,
with its tongue
to his face.

Bathymetry

On the sea, everything was different.
There were entire shoals of women-
pirates too, seawomen with their own
enforced sealaws, a choral, coral cure-
all for abuses they had suffered before.
In 950, great Lagertha, wild with hope,
speared through her own flopping husband.
A woman's anger is rarely taken seriously.
Pirates swore they saw mermaids roiling
under the water, but who did seawomen have
to desire? Did they dream of men so wild
for them that they gasped above the surface?
Or simply of men with kind eyes? Loving my
own bathymetry, I sometimes leave the potatoes
unwashed or the corn still streaked with hair —
wanting the wildness inside me, too.

How to Be the Other Woman

In the rock exhibit, the meteor
extinction is well-documented.
The signs of impact: shocked
quartz, spheres of weakened rock,
an unusual amount of irresponsible—

oh! of iridium. The red strata seam
like a stretch mark. We forget
to call this horror. The shards
could be passed off as jewels,
solemn in their spotlights.

When we are alone,
the ocean yowls outside.
We slide your ring across the table,
always pushing it away.
I call it a lizard's iris,
hold it up to my own face.
You say your wife is better

with metaphors.
The blush dogwood rails
at the window glass: take cover!
I flick out my tongue, slowly,
camouflage into the chair.

The Woman with Wounded Hands

For Nélida

Each morning you forget about
the layer of wood in your hands

forget the needle is ready to be plucked out
and used to sew a blouse in a factory

full of women who do not speak your language.
You forget that a particularly long sliver

makes an excellent stirrer for a pot of rice
or to skewer a fresh fish, whose eyes watch

you penetrate it from fin to nose.
You don't mind when the wounds

don't heal over because the shard
slides back in much easier that way.

Chicken Heart

In the blue dish, the knobbed plum
of a solitary chicken heart, which my mother
and her three sisters fight over. It is musky
and sweet and still tastes of blood.

It is funny the way in English
we call the cowardly chicken-hearted.

It is funny the way my mother takes
communion with her eyes open.

Crossing

My mother teaches me to float —
this one pool her entire world.

A spring peeper has been trapped,
crying from the mouth of the filter.

Grasses cling to the walls, like that peppered
water and soap experiment. Pushed out.

The parted prayer of the Nile, the crossing.

She comes eye to eye with the wailer.
To this bobbing rana: *Sana, sana.*

My mother stares at the frog as if trying
to become it, so easily unstuck,

so able to reach land.

Misplaced

I have to remember again
each morning. I try to think of
a morning that was clear.
I see my body everywhere, as if
I have misplaced it. My clavicle
is buried under the wilting
lilies by the sink. My hip bone gleams
under a stranger's coffee cup. My hands,
useless, appear all over the city.
I stop using exclamation points
because they are only for the living.
I cry when a rapist on the news is raped in prison.
I take primrose oil, which is good for "unbalanced
women." I wonder whether he is angry
that I left. I wonder whether he is glad
that I left. I change my mind.
I am here again each morning.

III

GOSPEL

Genesis

On the fifth day, the woman felt a cramp
in her rib and stroked it against a new
willow. Her side opened up: paper cut
blooming until she became paper doll—
split across x-axis until the front
of her held hands with the back, as they stood
beside one another, half-feet thrust into
thick freckled violets. A man emerged, too,
slick with extraterrestrial water, pressed her
gently back together. When God saw that
all was finished it leapt over their heads
in great snow leopard joy. And there was evening
and then apricot morning, and they smiled
at one another, having paused their gardening.

I Was Named for the
River of Blessings

I soon began to call my father by his own first name,
hoping to become good, which means halleluiah.

I cried out for a child like the Bible's Hannah, then him, named
after God itself. This baby body, slick with bright halleluiah.

The girls and I swapped stories about losing our virginities. I named
a man from a book. There are some firsts with no halleluiah.

On Sundays, I was busy with my work, crossing out the names
of the men in the hymnal. I sang only of my women, with *halleluiah*.

Yes, there were some men along the way. They could not name
me as I was. Not the kind ones, not the angry — never knowing halleluiah.

It's wanting in handfuls that keeps me here breathing. Naming
the exact way to be known, to be brought wildly to halleluiah.

There is another world, but I have already learned every rumbling name
of the breaththiefs in this one. I have learned, and can still cry halleluiah.

Bigger than I am, he touches each growing blackberry, naming
even the greenest ones. Oh, river of blessings. Oh halleluiah, halleluiah.

Upended

The sheets have been torn
into strips and the yucca has been left
unboiled in the pot
and the tarantulas have lost
legs protecting their young.
The butterfly jasmine has bent
itself at the very root to pay homage.
My mother's dress has slipped over her shoulder
but we are birthing babies here!
Who cares about a shoulder?
There is also blood on her cheek
but I do not tell her that
because it makes her look strong
in the way that I, at twelve,
want to be strong; in the way that
might confuse birth and death,
in the way you find yourself upended
into the underwater reflection
and simply keep stomping
through the mud.

Pilgrimage

Here is my mother, bright
against the night asphalt,
waltzing with the dress form
she pulled from its stand.

She named this torso Guadalupe
after the virgin mother,
who stayed good through every trial.
I look away as if

she's naked, although she's wearing
several coats at once.
I wonder what it's like to dance
with someone who cannot hold you.

It is snowing
and my mother has no shoes.
My father, too, watches
through the window, quiet.

Asymptote

My mother tells me my body is a temple.
I always forget about temples, unless a man
is burning one in the news. I know what the world
can do to a girl who only sees beauty in it.
Many things happen. In front of the school, I see
a man masturbate during lunch. And then the driver
who refuses to drive me home. And then the friend
who reenacts the poems I've shown him —
the saddest poems I've shown him. A man asks me
how I can stand to be touched at all, but I refuse
to die having not been pressed to someone
else's heart, having not come into the fullness of myself,
having not said this is my blood. This, my body. Saying no
or yes, and liking it.

Theodore Roosevelt Island

When you reach the island you will smell what you've learned
to call fish, but is just sweet rot. Run your fingers
through it as you might my hair, forgetting
how many sticks you have casually broken along
the way. Sweet man! do not forget to look down. See:
pine bark has crusted off like snakeskin, leaves of sea
glass, berries with green nipples, rocks blushed like kidneys,
sticks waiting patiently for their excavation,
an elephant foot stump, stones so pocked they may be
taut peach pits, a daddy long leg compound where the
leader has one very-long leg like men sometimes
have in their beards. You will see my prayer carved into
the cedar where I grooved your name so deep, will long
for me to taste the pulpy tree goodness with you.
Beloved, this is free for the taking.

Herding Tent Caterpillars

Each first week of April,
the caterpillars spin silk
tents in branches

of wild cherry
and crabapple trees.
The film spreads

morning by morning:
amniotic sac
of black squirm.

My father tastes them
brewing in the air.
The moment wakes him—

he who sleeps
through thunderstorms.
We strap black lamps

to our foreheads,
still gauzy with interrupted sleep.
Like fantastic germs

under a microscope
these giant bacterial bodies
web tree joints.

Unsettled, they pour
down to wriggle
on our outstretched arms

in great larval exodus
while we lumber after,
believing ourselves

commissioned by Pharaoh.
The crawl is deafening.

But the hand of God is with them and my father
catches us around our bellies.

Rejoice

And sometimes I think of the nights my mother lined us up
like eggs in a carton

to recite a chapter from Philippians
while we tap danced to discover the meaning of *rejoice*

which seemed then to be about the way my father kissed
his fingers after eating pork tenderloin

or the shimmer of sitting on the dock
with a brother and a dog

each eyeing the heel of bread you warned them
was for luring fish not feeding dogs and boys

who had yet to learn that rejoice might be
the way the attic fan feels in July

or something shattering
like discovering your name in a hymn in a hymnal

and having to sing it right then
to feel it reverberate your teeth with rightness

or watching a sky pinken and wanting to lick it
the way it feels to come eye to eye with a doe

and see her fold back down rather than run

This Is What the Girl Really Wants

I am neither God nor devil.
In the morning, I slice a pomegranate
and also my left palm. I cannot tell
which red is which, and because
I cannot tell, they are the same.
I do not know myself like this,
wet with something else's blood.
I want to tear my own hand away.
But the broken cups rest against the basin,
quiet and not asking anything of me.
I offer myself the washed fruit,
and accept it from myself.
The juice is just what I need.
This is what the girl really wants:
to be known as she is now.

Things to Cling To

For my siblings

You can still feel free when people love you,
knowing that all Chopin sounds red. Strong
teeth. A habit of spotting tiny things
and carrying them in your pocket.
You walk quickly to wherever
you are going even when you do not know
where you are going. You are not afraid
to stick your head through a dog door
and take a look around. Wearing raspberries
on your fingertips. Knowing that spider monkeys
only have four fingers and telling everyone.
That holiness is something that seems too real
for this world. Shadows that prove that there really is
something else, that men still look like children
when they sleep. Knitting dozens of crooked hats.
Baseball on the radio on summer nights.
The day at Abuela's when we went searching
for the good forks and found the dishwasher full
of unripe avocados. Your holiest laugh.
Tayberries, wineberries, olallieberries, salmonberries.

Liturgy

I want to say the same things over and over.
It is enough. Today is today. There will be
another fat sun and another fat moon.
You could not have saved that deer who
stared you down as she died on the highway.
Stand up from the top of your head.
Don't bother dusting the baseboards.
Throw out half cups of forgotten tea
and don't be ashamed of it. Lick kiwi
skins even though it's weird. Fold up
the shame like it's a fitted sheet. Carry
strawberry candies in your pocket.
Do the thing where you move from room
to room and feel like a different person
each time. Take a roadtrip with the man
who has aluminum cans on the floorboard.
Paint everything green, and then blue.
Say the winter will bleed into spring
and believe it to be true.

The Gospel According to the Girl

It is rolling in grass

until you're scratching at every curve.   The point is falling

in love with the beginnings of things.   The danger is letting the lukewarm

stay in your mouth.   Every girl should be told   she has an eternity

left to dance at sunset   so that she will waltz wildly

on the tongue   of the dock,   cha cha to her knees

in lakewater.

She buries herself   to the waist in the sandy mud,   always mid-slip

to a softer world   where she is just as she is now.

After dark, this tiny priest,   curtseying only to herself,   her lip sucked

into her mouth.   How do you teach a girl   to cling to everything good

of her mother   and none of the rest?   Do you ever stop watching

for her face to shine upon you?   This is how to dance

with another person, I tell her: to draw them closer,

to let them draw away.

JORDAN PÉREZ

works professionally in online safety

and childhood sexual abuse prevention.

She has an MFA in creative writing from

American University and has published poetry in *Cutthroat,*

Poetry International, Mississippi Review, and more.